# THE FEAST THAT STARVES

# THE FEAST THAT STARVES

JOANNA LABOUNTY

Hardcover ISBN: 979-8-9942684-0-7
Paperback ISBN: 979-8-9942684-1-4

# CONTENTS

*"Sunrise is my favorite,
it is the promise of a new day."*

For Olive and Bay
my lights, my loves, my happy.
May you always *thrive*.

Joanna LaBounty is a poet whose work began as therapy in ink and became a practice of reclamation. She writes of the body, survival, memory, and desire, where trauma and tenderness meet. She lives in Maine with her children and two rescue dogs. *The Feast That Starves* is her debut.

# I.

*Chasing The Light*

# FIREFLIES

Forever chasing fireflies
tiny lanterns darting
through early summer dark
twinkling Christmas lights
strung across the night sky.

Barefoot I dance
cool grass tickling my toes
I move too fast to think
hands flung wide
a child again
giggling,
grasping for the small, winged stars.

I miss, again and again,
but still I reach.

The chasing is the miracle.

And when, at last, I catch one
my palms glow
cupping its fragile fire
not to trap
not to dim the light
only to borrow its magic

to taste its glow
for a single breath
for a heartbeat,

before letting go.

# MOON MAN

Your Cheshire-cat smile
mocks me.
Oh, Moon Man,
why do you play these tricks?

I turn to you nightly
a whispered prayer
calling out a child's rhyme
casting you my dreams.

Seeking your brilliance
to illuminate
which way should I go?

A twinkle, a wink
before I slumber.

But you flood the dark
and cast only shadows
        laughing
oh, Moon Man.

show me.

# FIRST KISS

Your lips trembled when you kissed me,
tiny earthquakes of nervousness.
I placed my hand on your face,
reassuring you it was okay.

When you asked me if I was too,
I giggled.
Sure I am,
I'm just cooler than you.

You laughed out loud
and kissed me deeply
like it was forever,
and for a second
I believed in forever too.

# LOVE

Live with me.
Love with me.
Knife-tip prick
bleed for me.

Try with me.
Confide in me.
Fairy-dust, iron-rust,
believe in me.

Trust in me.
Hold some fucking respect
for me.

Be near me.
See with me.
See what the future,
our future,
could dare to hold for me.

Pray with me.
Stay with me
but only,
only,
if you've got love for me.

Ride with me.
Have pride in me.
Get drunk on me.
Moonshine, baby, burn for me.

Ash and ember,
rise with me.
See the strength,
see the fight,
see the fire inside of me.

Live with me.
Love with me.

# MORNING DEW

The earth
she lies in balance
movement and stillness.
Steadily breathing,
inhaling, exhaling the wind.

Long wisps of her hair
stretched out,
freely, wild.

The rise and fall of her chest,
the curves,
the hills, valleys, and mountains
glimpsed only in passing,
half-hidden
beneath the fog-blanket
that clings to her.

The soft, sweet smell of grass
and her morning dew
stirs him.

He is awake.
Even veiled,
he knows her shape,
her rhythm,
her breath
he knows her scent
he knows her depth

The home his body remembers.

# II.

## *The Feast That Starves*

# THE KING OF NOTHING

You feast,
the phony king at the head of the table.

*Wench, bring me more!*

Teeth tear flesh,
grease slick on lips.
You devour like a beast,
jaws unhinging

I heap your plate,
refill your glass
    more bread, more meat,
     more pie, more wine.

You gorge,
I wither.

A pup, waiting,
tail wagging,
begging for scraps,
surviving only
on the bones you toss.

A feast that starves,
and still
you call yourself king.

# THE RED DOOR

The wooden frame shattered
from your fight.
Fragments scattered
splinters across the welcome mat
they cut my soles,
they cut my soul.

I bleed footprints
across the threshold.

You came with fists
shouting words
a loaded gun.

You broke everything you touched.

The cold February draft
rushes in,
howling through the gaps,
wolves hungry for blood.

Snow slips through,
your footprints frozen in time.
Bloody handprints for wallpaper,
wall-to-wall screams,
a house haunted
by the unwelcome guest.

But you thought the splinters
could silence me?

The sun,
she always rises,
no serpent strong enough
to keep her swallowed.

Relentless, she lays her light
across the wreckage.
She threads the fractures in stars,
and what you left behind
guides me through the dark.

# COOK

I cook,
my love served,
sauce on the plate,
my heart, my soul,

sprinkled, seasoned, poached.

But you do not taste it.
You starve yourself,
call it my fault.
You toss it,
spoil it,
spit it out
and call it poison.

I burned my fingers,
blistered my tongue,
and still -
you taste nothing.

# THANKFUL

A heartbreak is never even,
wishbone snapped,
and I won the bigger half.

Cracked bone
pierced my palm,
tiny blood droplets fall
on the white tablecloth
stained
before the vows were kept.

The burden of the prize.

Still, I try to be thankful.

But the bone was picked clean,
left to dry out,
a broken parting gift
at the end of the meal.

And you,
already reaching
for something sweeter,
your next bite.

I sit alone with the mess,
left to clean it up.

No wishes left to make.

# DRUNK

I am at the bottom
of the bottle you drown in,
empty as the glass
you refill.

It never quenches
your thirst.

Clink of ice cubes
frosts my heart.

The hands that once held me
wrap tightly around the cup.
Your lips kiss the rim,
over and over,
your vision blurs,
no longer seeing me

and I float
away.

# III.

## *Threads*

# SWEATER

When did the thread pull?
The sweater is quickly unraveling.

What was once woven
 a bold, beautiful pattern
 is now a tangled mess,
 yarn in knots.

Can it be mended?

Fisherman's knit
knots crossing, *not* crossing,
impossible now
to trace which line was yours
and which was mine.

My calloused fingers
cannot weave it
alone.

# THE DARK KNIGHT

you became my obsession,
 the one who got away,
 the dark knight,
 the guiding light,
 the love I craved,
 the love I hungered for,
 the love I longed for.


your indifference was torture.


every sugar-sweet love song,
every fucking lovesick movie,
every shooting star,
every birthday candle,
    every fortune cookie daydream -
                it was you
You.
You.
You.


I had to purge you,
two fingers down my throat,
bile rising,
gagging on goodbye,
 bent over the sink,
spitting out your name
saltwater rinse
to finally breathe
without the taste of you
on my lips.

# TRASH

How did it feel?
To use my body,
then discard it,
tossed in the trash.

Do you still think of my flesh?
Does it rot inside you?
Does it bring you pleasure?

You wanted my chest,
your hands clenched my breasts,
but not the heartbeat
behind them.

Vultures circling
you fed on my hunger.

You told me to fall to my knees.
You called it worship,
but it was desecration.

Despite my prayers,
you were never saved.
There was no salvation.
No rest for your wicked.

My mouth was good for something,
praised for its sweet lips
until words came out.
You wanted nothing
to do with those.

Wasted.
Used.
Discarded.

# THE SILENT MOVIE

You loved me most
when I followed you around,
smiled pretty,
but didn't make a sound.

I screamed into the silence
until my throat was raw,
until the walls bent inward,
until my breath was afraid
of being seen.

How many times
did you tell me to leave?

Four.

And now you are standing there,
asking me
why I walked out the door?

We are not actors
in your silent film.
Choreographed,
lost in the subtitles.
Fade to black.
Cut the scene.

# HOMEFRONT

I didn't ask for war
 I asked for a home.

Warrior wasn't the role I wanted.
 I wanted to be a wife.

But the battlefield came anyway
 bloodshed,
 shrapnel from broken vows,
 bullet holes
 instead of baked goods
 and bedtime routines.

I waved the white flag -
 Did you not see it?

I tried to surrender to softness.

Battle cries,
 battling cries.

I never wanted the armor,
 the sword,
    the war.

# IV.

## *What We Inherit*

# MOM

Her voice in my head is loud,
the kind that grows
from the weight of silence.

Her breath
Marlboros and cheap boxed wine,
a blend that clings,
seeping into walls,
seeping into me.

Her words stained everything:
lipstick ghosts on glasses,
wine rings on the table,
ash drifting down,
settling into the curtains.

The air itself
reeking of neglect.

"I got an A in class today, Mom."
"Good for you, now, pour me another."

I tipped the box forward,
just as she taught me,
to wring the last drop
from the foil throat.

"Aren't you proud of me?"

A flick of the lighter replies,
 a grin flashed with yellow teeth,
 a pink smear of lipstick on her smile.

And still,
 the smoke clings,
 splashed wine bleeds through the wood.

Some stains never come out in the wash.

# MY SHADOW

My trauma is my shadow.

On the days
 when the sun is highest,
 brightest,
 you cannot see it
 not until I lift my foot,
 take a step forward.

But when the sun sinks low,
 the shadow lengthens,
 a distorted version of myself
 stretching beyond my own shape,
 dwarfing me.

It twists, contorts,
 warps the edges of me
 until I cannot recognize
 the figure following me home

# HOPSCOTCH

My dad's fists, my mom's words
stones thrown on numbered squares
rules were simple
don't wobble, don't cry
don't land where you shouldn't

hot concrete skinned knees
chalk-dust palms
playground shouting everywhere

one foot down one foot lifted
a child between rules and chaos

monkey bar arms burning
pretending I could fly
swings pumping higher higher
orbit nearly mine

kickball became dodgeball
*ouch*
**you are out**

tag taught me
safety always moved
the second I reached it

survive survive
until
the bell
yells

# V.

## *Heat in the Body*

# BLINDNESS

And you were there,
 every fucking time I closed my eyes
 the image of you
 tattooed on my eyelids.

Blink.

I wanted to scratch, to claw,
 to tear you out,
 erase the sight of you forever.

Blindness.

But most often,
 on nights blanketed in dark,
 I found myself
 pressing my palms deep into my lids,
flesh to flesh
 longing for nothing more
 than to be close to you
 once more.

# TATTOOS

Timid fingertips,
walk the curve of my hip,
carefully luring me in,
making distance disappear.

The swirls and grooves
of your fingerprints
press through thin fabric,
meeting the lines of ink,
tattoos on my skin.

I hope those fingers
learn to color outside the lines,
press harder,
blur the edges,
smudge the ink,
until heat seeps through,
until my skin swells,
until the art comes alive
alive beneath your hands.

# MY SUMMIT

Crumbled sheets
become mountains and valleys
creating a vast distance
between us
I head out on my expedition
the touch of your skin,
my summit

# DESIRE

I want
the rough of your hands
tangled in the silk of my hair.

I want
the gruff of your voice,
breaking into whisper,
spilling goodnights
across the pillowcase.

The bite of your kisses
on the soft of my neck,
my flesh.

The rush of you
slow,
so slowly.

# TELL ME

Your voice,
gravel,
full of certainty, demand,
the one rooms lean toward

But in the dark
I hear it catch,
a half-breath,
something caught in your teeth?
Have you only practiced
those words in your sleep?
Commands like matches
struck in a closed fist,
the small blue flame
no one was meant to see?

It burns...
          fantasy

Is it fear
of finally allowing
that door to open wide?

Say it.
Welcome it in.

Let the authority
step out of its armor
unsheathed, unleashed

Tell me where to be.
If your voice shakes,
I will hold the tremor.
If your gaze drops,
I will lift it.

You can stand
And boy,  I know how to kneel

Ask, and I am there,
thirsting for your hunger,
laid down
your shadow over me,
my mouth open to your requests,
a yes answering yes.

Just tell me.

# THE STORY

I want to be
the sunrise after a starless night,
to make the corners of your eyes crinkle,
your heart race,
your palms go damp.

I want to be
the reason for your messy bed,
your late-night hungry calls,
your wandering thoughts,
your daydreams.

I want to be
the giggle that erupts,
the first thought with good news,
the soft pillow for sleepy heads,
the twinkle in the night sky,
the dance you never want to end.

I want to be
the hand you reach for,
the book you dog-ear the pages of,
the story you carry
with you, always.

# VI.

*Salt and Stillness*

# SAILBOATS

I adjust my sails,
fabric stretched and billowed,
edges frayed,
battered,
wind-whipped, chafed raw.

I changed course.
The destination
no longer mattered.

Maps torn and scattered,
I crave the stillness
of the sea.

# TULIPS

spring tulips
delicate ballerinas
on pointed toes
leaping gracefully
into the light of spring

# SING

Windows down,
wing out.

I sing
not the longing cry
of the loon on the lake,
but the soft, sweet chirps
of early spring birds.

Truck in drive,
wind-wild hair,
the road my chapel,
the beat my prayer.

Forward.

# INKWORK

I wrote my story
in ink and needles,
chapters carved
where scars once lived.

Every mark a witness:
lines for the losses,
shadows for the nights
that almost ended me.

Words etched in black:
  *Be Brave*
to remind me
that fear is not the end.

A forest,
dark and twisting,
branches reaching
like hands in the night
the places I wandered,
almost lost,
and the path I found my way out.

My children,
stitched in like vows,
together we thrive,
olive and bay,
reminders that love
is the only legacy worth leaving.

My hawk,
high priestess,
guiding light,
wings stretched wide
along my hip,
eyes sharp
to catch what is unseen,

My phoenix,
rising,
rebirth seared into my skin
proof that ashes
are not the last chapter.

The canvas reclaimed.
I chose this pain,
I chose the permanence.

Declarations, not decorations.
My body is mine
artwork, defined.

# SIREN

Long silver strands
cascade like waterfalls
over the swell of my breasts,
a crown of tides,
moon-pulled, untamed.

Sweetly singing to sailors,
hips swaying with the surf,
lips curved,
serenade spun on salt air
an invitation,
a dare.

Soft lines etch the map
of every laugh,
 of every loss,
the tides I have weathered,
the storms I have outlasted.

Lighthouse eyes,
a beacon,
fixed and steady,
a promise of home
to those who do not fear my fire.

I love her
this body of mine,
not delicate like a pressed flower,
but sea-born,
steady,
shaped by storms,
forever dancing in the spray.

Like the pearl
that formed
in the grit of the oyster,
 layer after layer,
 luminous from the struggle
                    the treasure I've become.

# HOME

I painted the door pink
softer, lighter
than the red door that was broken.

This home is mine.
Ours.

We spill here,
 shout-sing,
 kitchen dance party here.

We fill the walls with art,
 the air with laughter,
 the cupboards with food.

We entertain here.
We make a beautiful mess here.
We play games,
construct pillow forts,
dine at the table covered in scars.

We make memories here.

This house is our home,
roots
after a lifetime
        floating like dandelion tufts
                    on the wind.